THE ART OF KARATE

空手道の芸術

THE ART OF
KARATE

Shihan Tak Kubota
President, International Karate Association

Photography

Mark Miller

HADDINGTON
HOUSE

a division of Peebles Press International, Inc.

First Published 1977 by
Peebles Press International, Inc.
10 Columbus Circle, New York, New York 10019

Designed by The Pacific Coast Creative Company
Corona del Mar, California

© 1977 Peebles Press International, Inc.

ISBN 0-672-52332-9

Library of Congress Catalogue Card Number 76-53591

Distributed by
The Bobbs-Merrill Co., Inc.
4300 West 62nd St., Indianapolis, Indiana 46268, U.S.A.
in the United States and Canada

Barrie & Jenkins
24 Highbury Crescent
London N5 1RX, England
in the U.K., Ireland, Australia, New Zealand and South Africa

Printed and bound in the United States of America

Introduction

I would first like to say that I am extremely pleased to be associated with this project because, for the first time, a very large audience can view the subject of karate as it should be displayed—as an art form.

This is a picture book—a photographic perception of the beauty, the grace, the commitment, the spirit of karate. It is intended to portray a side of karate that is rarely seen, an aspect removed from the "scream-at-everybody, kill-everything" image so readily displayed in motion pictures and television and different from the approach found in static how-to-do-it defense technique booklets which are heavily laden with diagrams and verbiage.

This book is for the purist and can hopefully be likened to a photo essay on ballet in that the camera lens was utilized in the same manner—to freeze the moment of meaningful movement, to show how each single motion not only plays a part in a total progression, but has a special, and often spiritual, meaning and beauty all its own.

Millions of people all over the world are familiar with karate as a means of self-defense, as a sport, but the layman knows little of the ancient traditions and disciplines that have been passed down from Master to student through the ages. These same precepts act as the guiding philosophies of modern karate. You will see that several of these ancient thoughts appear within the book.

Again, for the purists, I have written in my own hand the Japanese characters, presented along with English translations, which describe the occurrence in each of the photographs. I have also provided a glossary of significant terms which can be found in the appendix section.

What follows is a brief history of karate—very brief because this is not a history book. Then, over 200 pages of art...the graceful evolution of the spiritual and physical being with emphasis first on the individual and his deeply personal commitment and progressing to his involvement with others. Behold...the *Art of Karate*.

Shihan Tak Kubota

History

In its beginning, karate was simply an unorganized, purely physical method of self-defense. Its practitioners had little time for philosophizing about the art and looked upon its techniques solely as a means of survival. The Oriental definition of the word "karate" meant "China hands" in deference to karate's heritage. As the techniques and usage of karate progressed, or perhaps as society progressed, the experts (also known as Shihans or Masters) of this violence began to look for greater meaning in what they did as it became apparent that there was less need to fight just to survive. Also, Zen Buddhism was emerging as an important religious influence which ultimately became the guiding force of the spirit of karate.

In 1935, Gichin Tunakoshi, one of the Masters of that period, changed the Oriental symbol for "karate" to read "empty hand". This reinforced the fact that karate was an unarmed self-defense and promoted the Zen Buddhist meaning of emptiness, i.e. if a person intends to develop completely he must first "empty" his soul. This was the beginning of the transformation of Karate-Jitsu, of Karate-do, the way of karate, the art of karate.

Creed of the International Karate Association

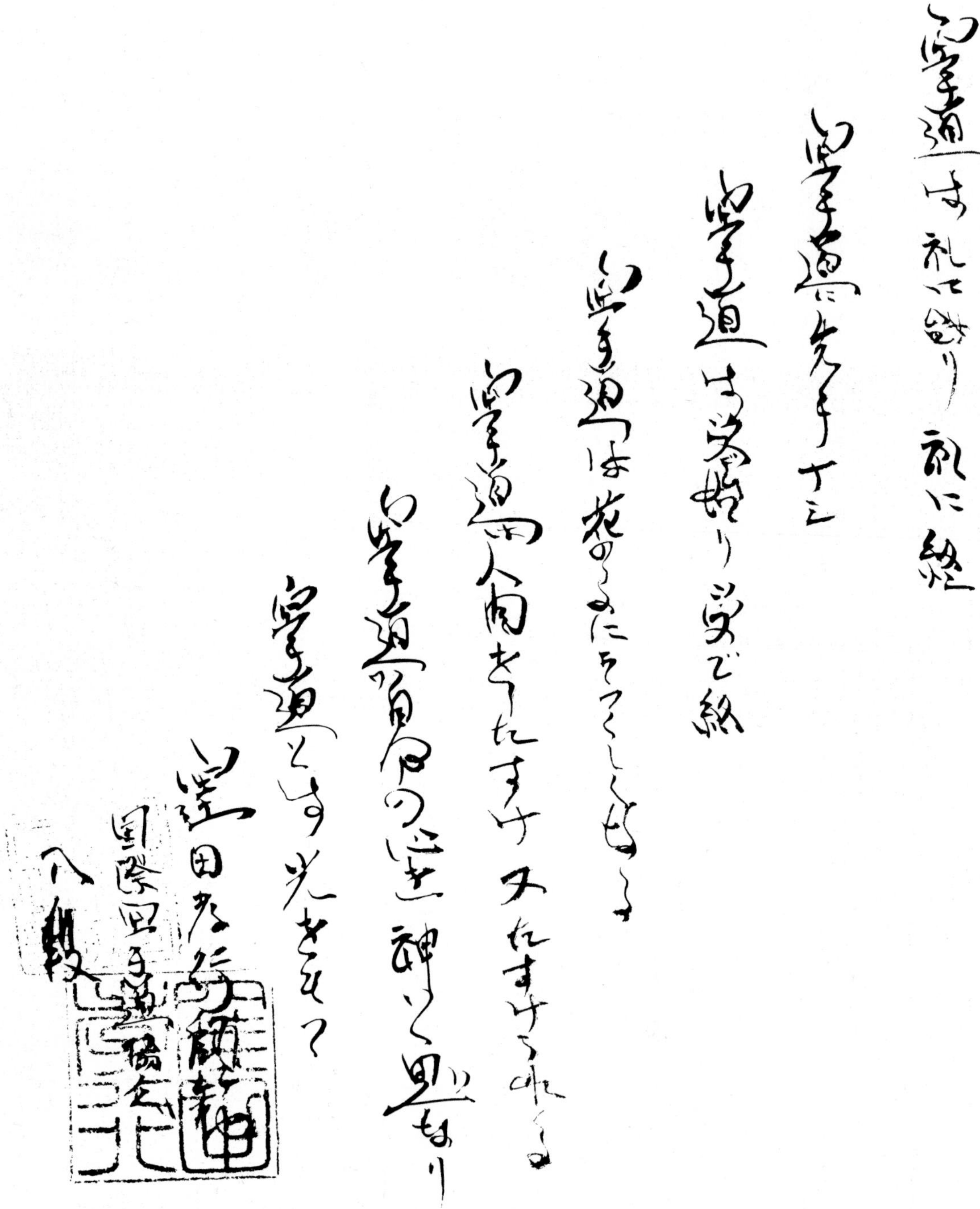

空手道は礼に始り礼に終る

空手道先手なし

空手道は義の補り助で終

空手道は花より心つくし行ふ

空手道人間きたすけたすけられる

空手道頃の空神く思なり

空手道とす光きそて

空手名行　頃も　国際空手連盟を　人形段

1. Karate begins and ends with respect.
2. Always start with meditation to clear the mind of all thoughts save karate.
3. Movements start with defense and end with defense.
4. Karate is like a flower...sometimes soft, sometimes fierce.
5. Karate is a brotherhood where each owes his help to the other.
6. The power of karate comes from the God within.
7. The true karate man exudes an aura of power which others sense instinctively.

"The essence of karate is the spirit...the unity of body and soul."

空道の手刀と師範の顔

SHUTO TO SHIHAN NO KAO
The master's face concentrates on killing the enemy

空 の 剛 の 力

KARATE NO GO NO CHIKARA
Body tension

KARATE-DO TO YARI
When attacking you must bear only one thing in mind — kill the enemy...
One will never be defeated when fighting with this attitude

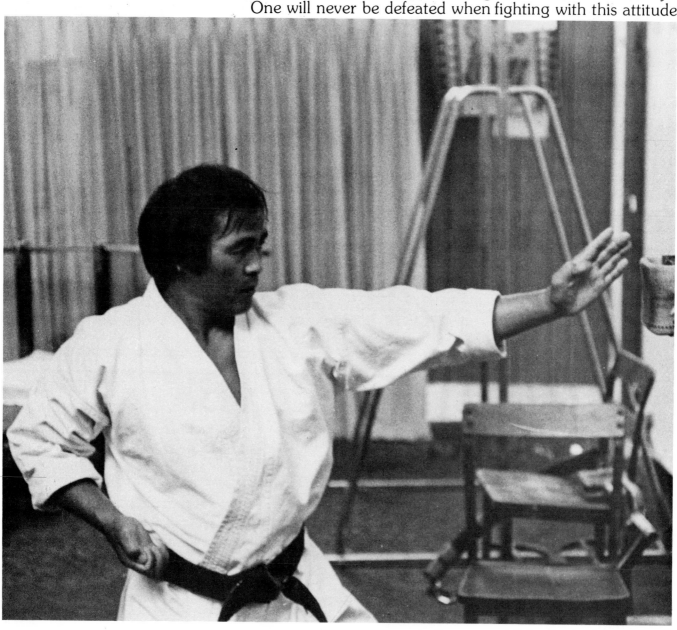

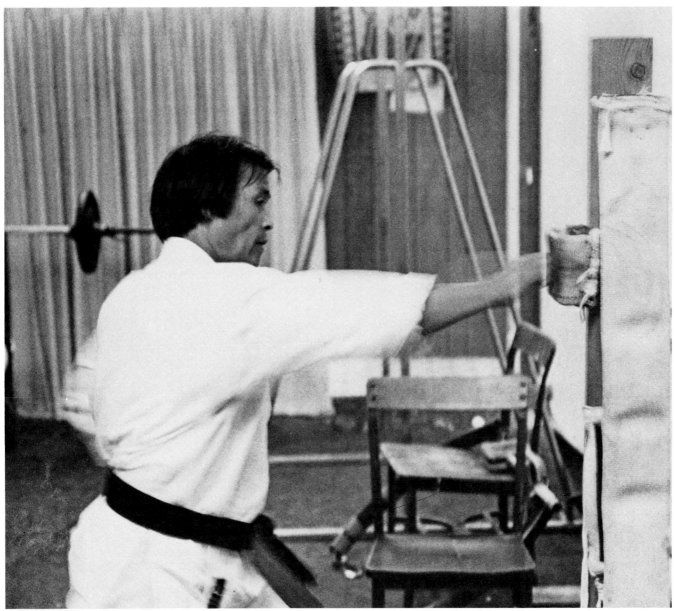

HIRA KEN
Forefinger knuckle strike

空手道の心

KARATE NO KOKORO
The spirit of the karate brush

筆の黙想

FU DE NO MOKUSO
Concentration on the brush

"I am in my Master's shadow...I *am* my Master's shadow."

DOJO NO SOJI
Scrubbing the dojo floor (Teaches respect for the dojo)

少年と空手道

自分も黒帯になりたい

"KURO-O-BI NI NARITAI"
"I want to learn to be a black belt"

KI-AI
Shout, yell

KARATE NO ASHI CHIKARA NO ASHI
Power is derived from a rooted stance

空道気合前屋文

KI-AI NO OIZUKI
Charging forward with a yell and punch

SEIZA MOKUTO
Sitting meditation

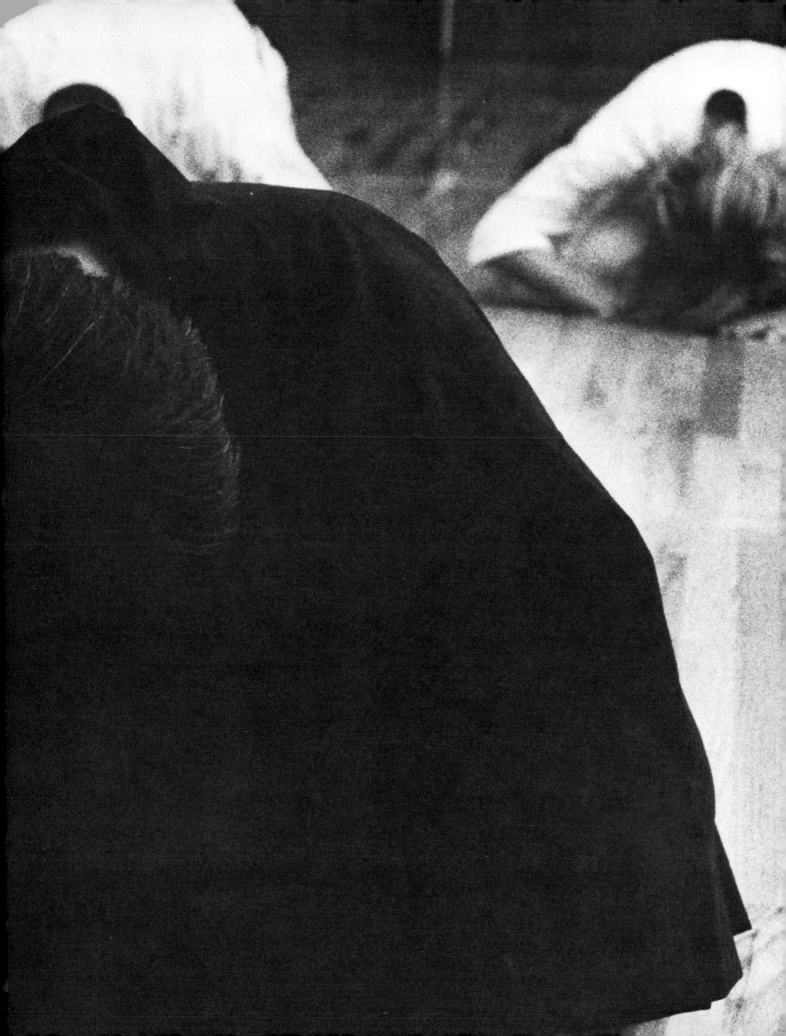

"The meaning of karate is...empty hand."

HIRA KEN
Forefinger knuckle

空手道々後屈立

KOKUTSU DACHI
Backward stance with a downward block

KI-AI
Shout, yell (Attack to the side)

奥多道の艾

UKE
Side defense

KARATE NO MOKUTO DE TSUKI
Meditating an attack

UKE
Crossed arm blocking

書道の心の友

TSUKI
Punching outward

四ノ段ノ稽古ノ受

CHUDAN KIZAMI TSUKI
Punch to the midsection, starting with a fake

空の光の受

KARATE NO HIKARI UKE
"Sunlight defense" Openhanded blocking

空手道の影

KARATE-DO NO KA GE
Vibrations of power

KARATE TO UMI
Karate on the ocean

空と空手道の～力

空手道 究

KARATE-DO TSUKI
To be capable of striking in all directions

KARATE NO CHIKARA
Power through body tension

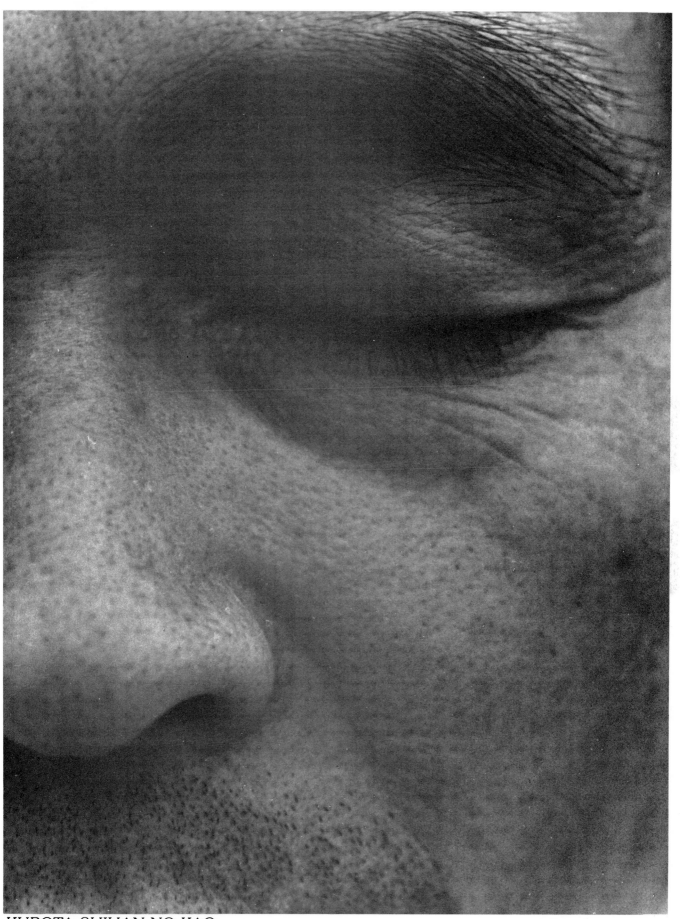

窪田師範のく顔、

KUBOTA SHIHAN NO KAO
The face of the Master Kubota in meditation

空道の心の黙想

KOKORO NO MOKUSO
Developing the spirit through meditation

"True knowledge of karate cannot be taught...it can only be explained through technique or through metaphor..."

GYAKU ZUKI
Reverse punch to the midsection

UMI NO SUNA DE YOKOGERI
Side kick training in the sand

GO NO UKE
Defense through body tension

SHUTO KARA NO UKE
Openhanded outward defense

x

URA-KEN
Striking with a hammer fist

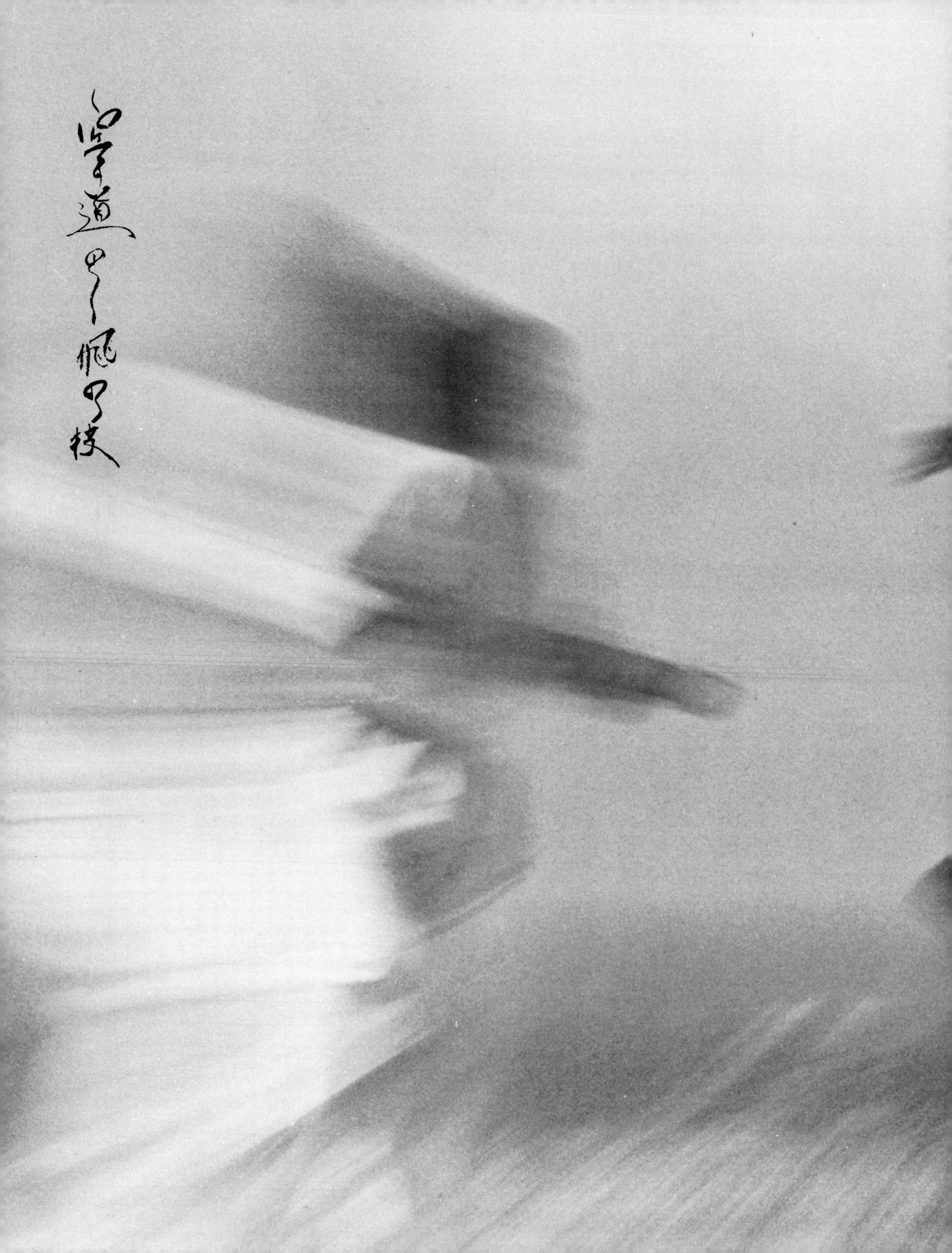
学道の風の様

TOBI WAZA
The technique of jumping through space

山崎道の横蹴

YOKO GERI
Side kick

空手道は花のように心を鍛える

HANA NO YO NI KOKORO-O KITA-ERU
The experience of a flower as a discipline toward becoming aware of the true self

"The traditions of karate are practiced in the katas or technique forms which perfect the grace, consciousness, and power of the physical self and spirit."

空手道の芸術

KARATE NO GEI JITSU
Structured forms from the laws of the universe

空と空手道

SORA TO KARATE-DO
The spirit of karate is also the heavens

空手道の空の飛

SORA TO KARATE-DO
The experience of one's space is on the path of karate

空に空手道二段蹴

The sky becomes the opponent in the practice of a double kick

空手道默想

KARATE-DO MOKUSO
Meditation: the physical universe

SHUTO UCHI
Knife hand strike

五段の型

GO DAN NO KATA
Down block in a back stance in the fifth form

空手の上段と下段の～受

KARATE JYODAN TO GEDAN NO UKE
Up and down block

空手の突の〜黙想

KARATE NO TSUKI NO MOKUSO
Concentration punch, achieved through meditation

空手のしば前一突

KARATE NO SHIKO DACHI NO UKE
Inside knife block

85

MIZU NO KATA
Kata developed in water reflection

空手道之水

MIZU
Moving through water to strengthen oneself

空手道水蹴

MIZU KERI
The challenge of kicking through water

墨書の心　水里心の力

MIZU NO KOKORO NO CHIKARA
The essence of water and the power of the self are one and the same

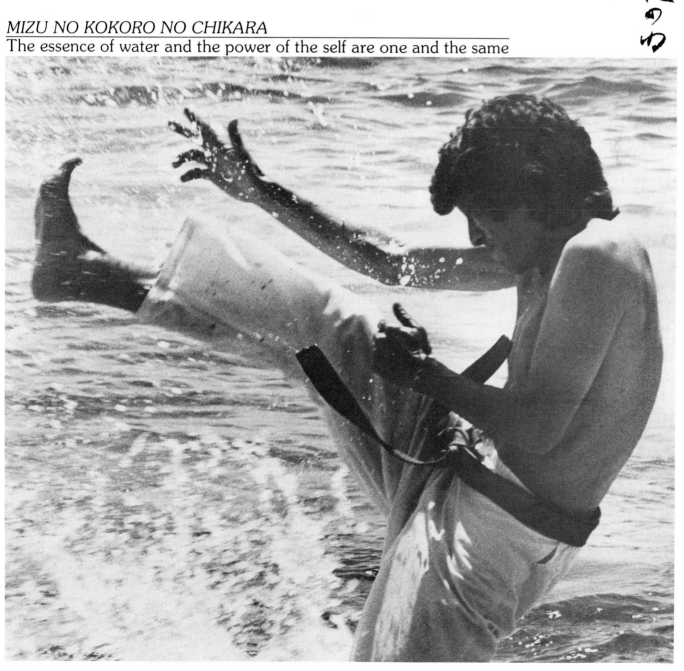

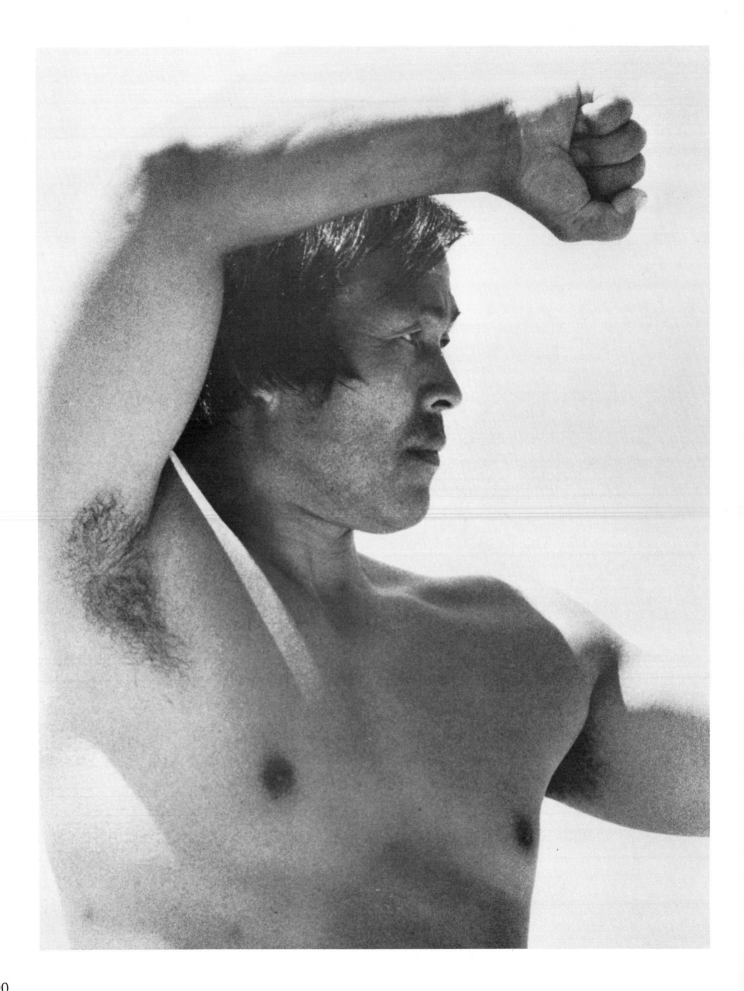

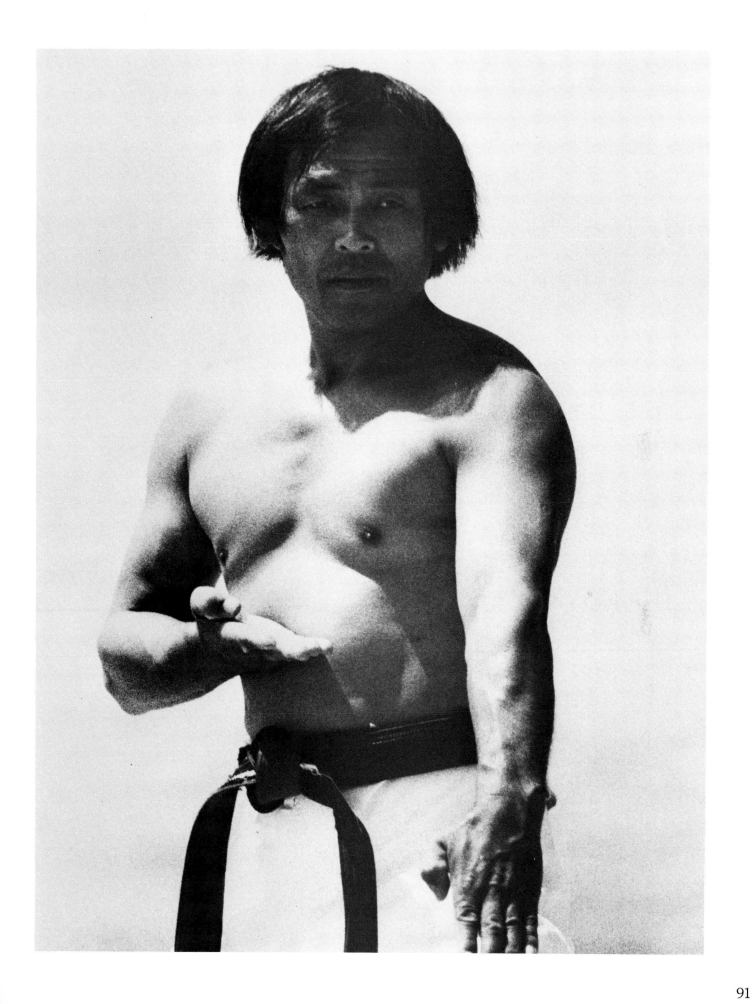

目の体

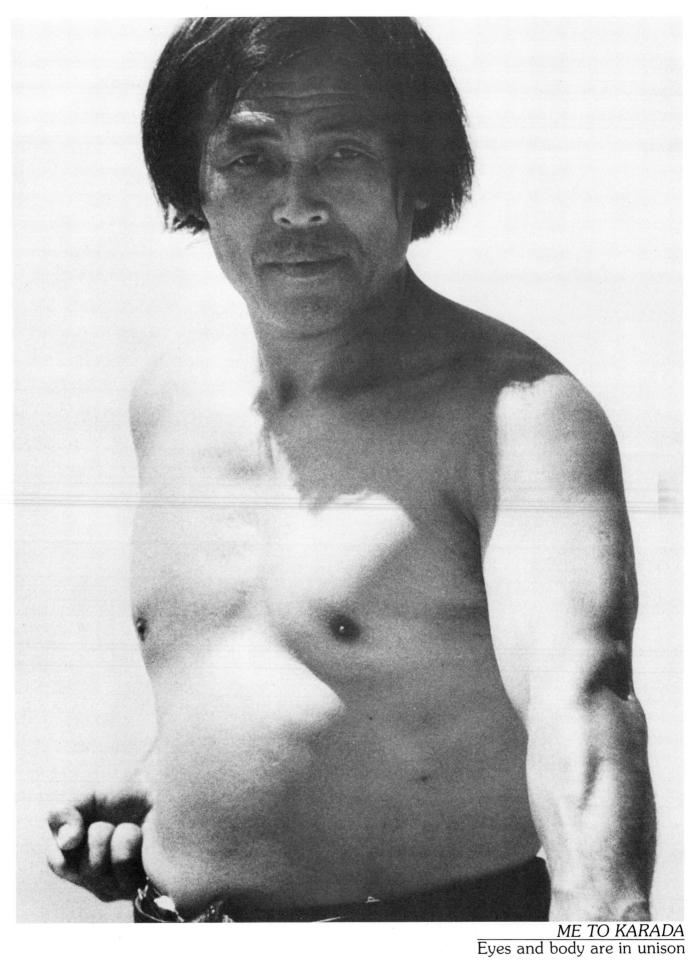

ME TO KARADA
Eyes and body are in unison

写真道の変化

KARATE-DO NO TSUKI TSUKI
Karate isn't one way but many ways

CHIKARA NO NUKITE
The simultaneous thrust of the fingertips

KARATE-DO TO I CHI TO NINGEN
Blocking and punching training must be as concentrated
as a rock and as endless as the sky

UKE NO KATA
Blocking form

GEDAN NUKITE
The fingertips as weapons can be directed toward the lower section of the opponent and the eyes of an attacker coming from behind

NINGEN NO HIKARI
There is a level of purpose in karate that manifests
itself as an "aura" which cannot be seen or touched—
It is sensed...No one would dare attack

奥儀 上段突

JYODAN TSUKI
Attack to the face

JYODAN TSUKI
The moment of an attack to the opponent's face is timeless

KARATE-DO NO MOKUTO
Concentration to develop the spirit to attack

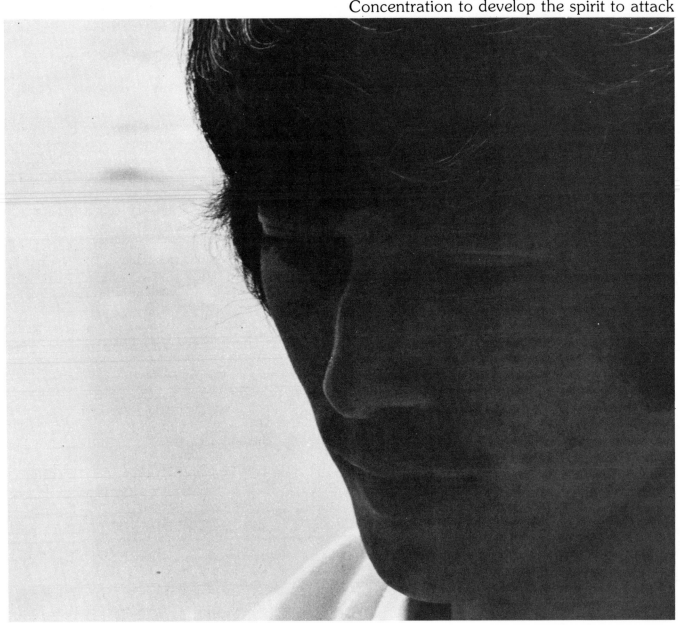

"To truly know karate, one must experience it along the path of the Master. By following the Master, the student learns perfection of life and discovers the search for true spirit..."

空手道の人間の目

KARATE-DO NO NINGEN NO ME
To each his viewpoint of his experience, to all the common path their goal

SORA NO YONI KOKORO O KITAERU
Strengthening of the physical self

自分の心を　砥のようにみがやく指導

JIBUN NO KOKORO O SUNANO
YONI NAGARERU SHIDO
Truth flows like sand

空手道の中段の気合

CHUDAN NO KI-AI
All power is lost unless you perfect what is known as
KIAI, joining of the body and soul

KARATE-DO NO KOKORO NO UKE
Practicing of all blocks is mandatory for proficiency in one

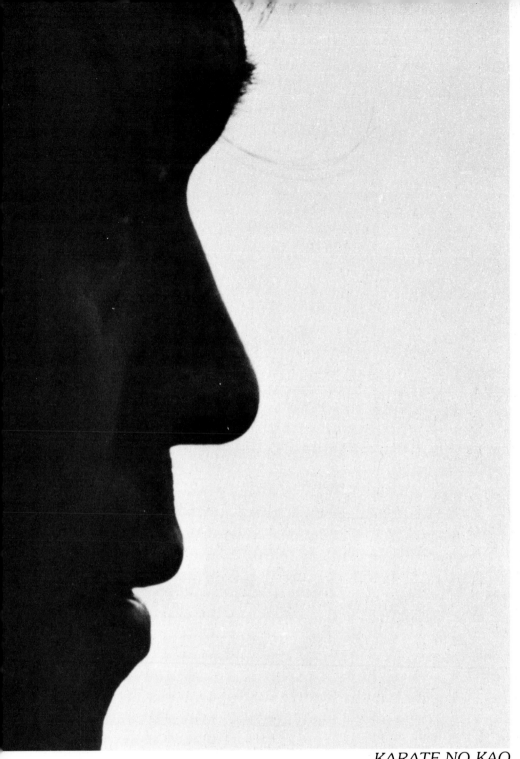

空手道の顔、

KARATE NO KAO
The visage of the Master

空手道の四段の型

YODAN NO KATA
The first movement of the fourth form

空手道之海

KARATE-DO TO UMI
Karate reflected in ripples of water has shape

UKE NO SHIDO
Teaching to block

KARATE-DO NO KATA
Following the Master's form

松

120

CHUDAN KOKUTSU UKE
Back stance defense against an attack to the midsection

空手道の山突

YAMA ZUKI
Half punch with inward body tension

空手道 平和の外受

126

KUMI TE NO KATA
Form will develop free style

空手道の型の受

KARATE-DO NO KOGEKI
Following the spirited charging attack

GODAN NO KATANO TOBI KERI
The fifth of many forms (jumping)

KOGEKI
Attacking

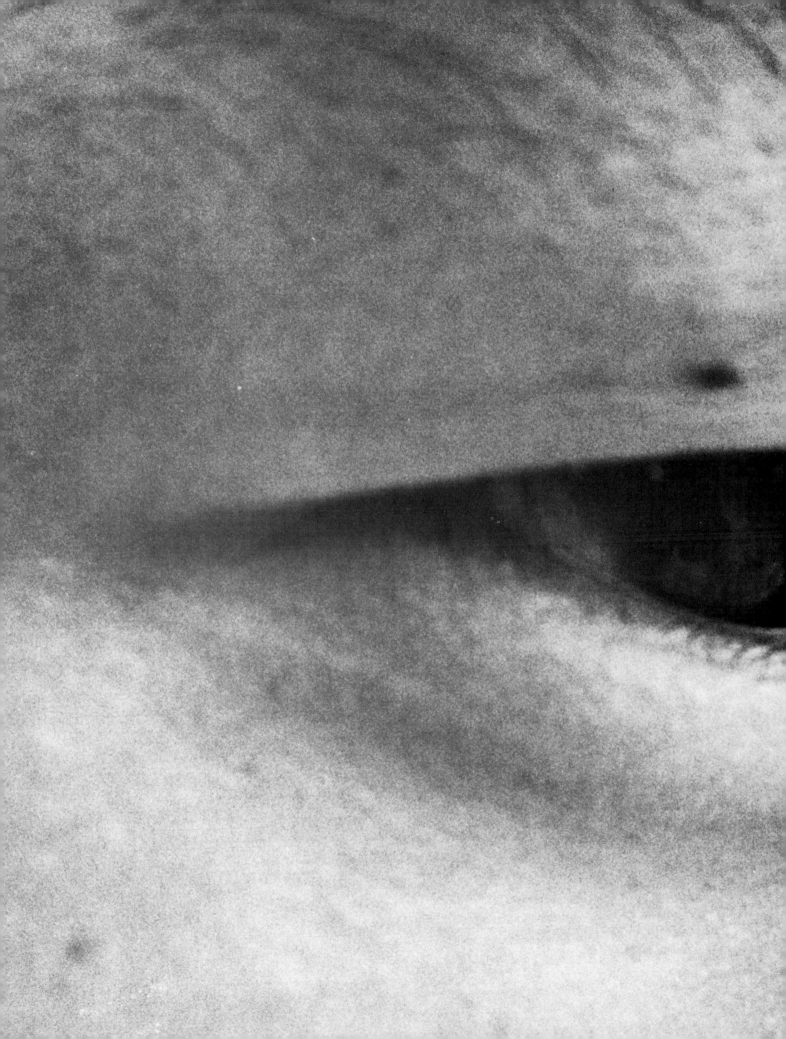

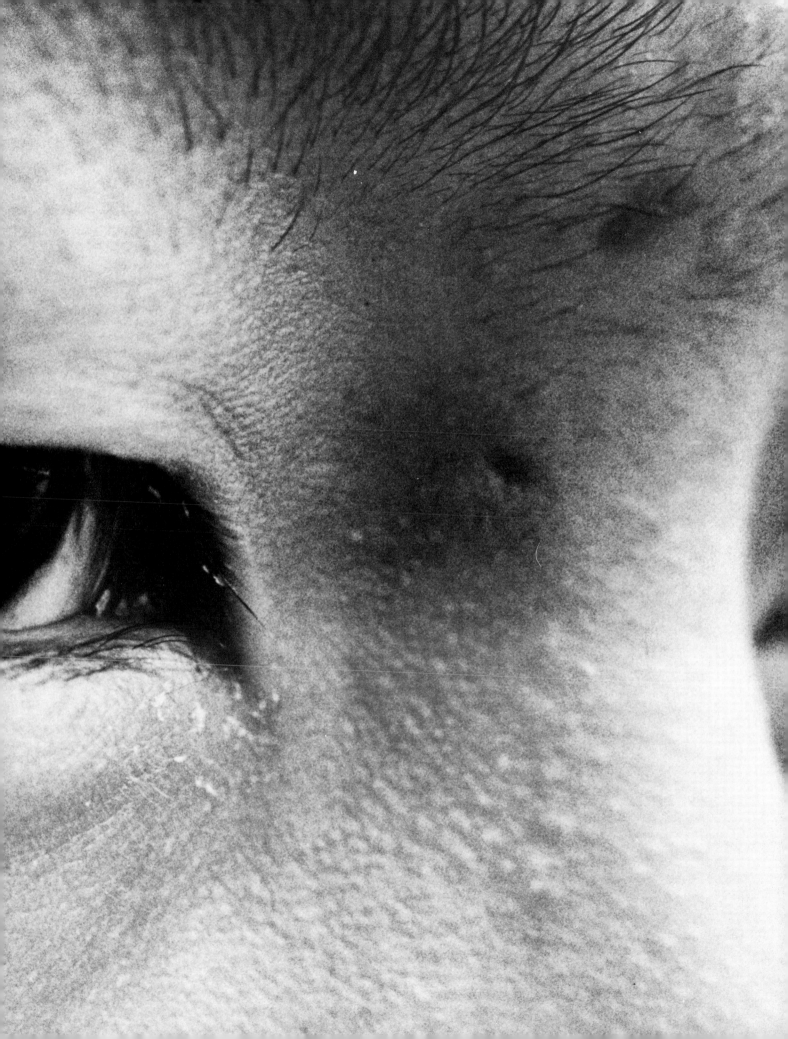

"In the eyes of the novice, the face of the Master is the face of karate...the determination to win, whatever the challenge."

空手道の組手

KARATE-DO NO KUMITE KATA
Seeking the techniques of combat

AIKI-DO NO UKE
Techniques include aikido defenses

空手道の攻撃

140

合気道受

AIKI-DO NO UKE
Aikido defense in which the attacker's own force is used against him

NAGE NO WAZA
Aikido defense is completed with an effortless throw

空手道の心や行

KOKORO WA YUKU
The body and spirit must go together

空手道の型の横蹴

KATA NO YOKOGERI
Side thrust kick to face

146

空手道乃型

KARATE-DO NO KATA
KONKU SHO, a black belt kata

空手道の平手

HIRA TE
Knife hand

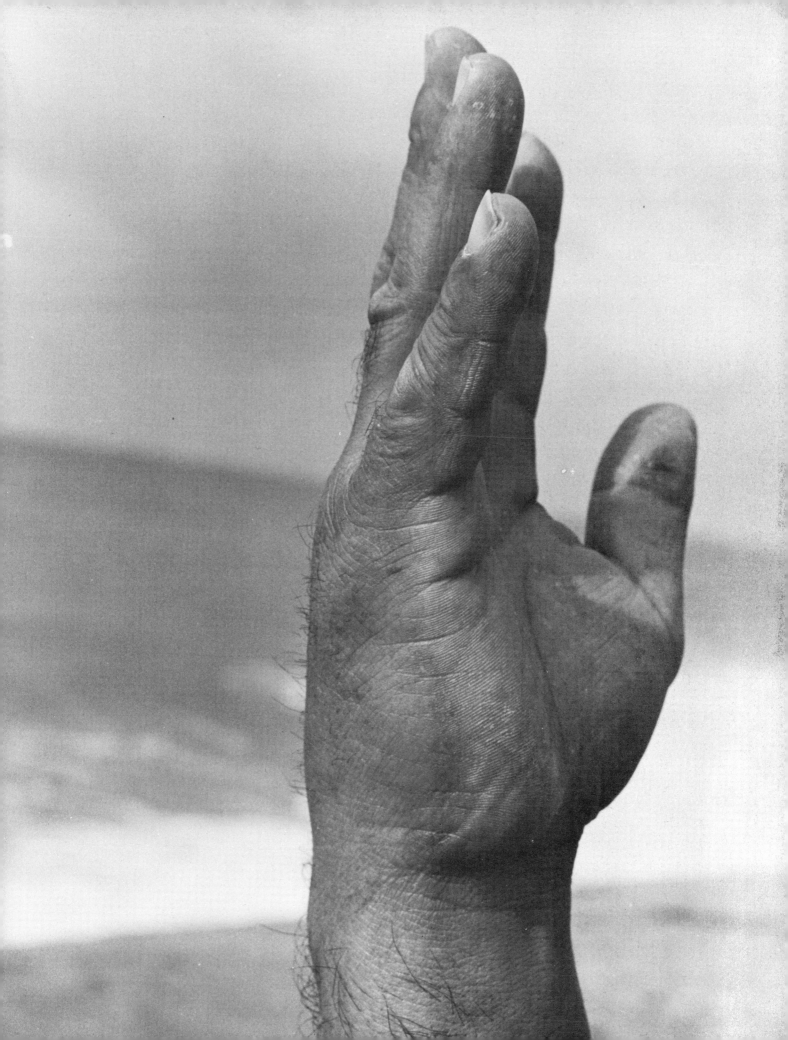

JYODAN UKE
Face block

手を見る目

TE O MIRU ME
Watching the hand of your attacker

上段突かう蹴

JYODAN UKE KARAKERI
Blocking face punch and counterattack with a kick

六段蹴

JYODAN GERI
Face kick

SAI NO UKE
Defense with a SAI, which is thought of as an extension
of the arm rather than as a weapon

手を掴む顔

TE-O-TSUKAMU KAO
Ultimate power derived through melding of body and mind

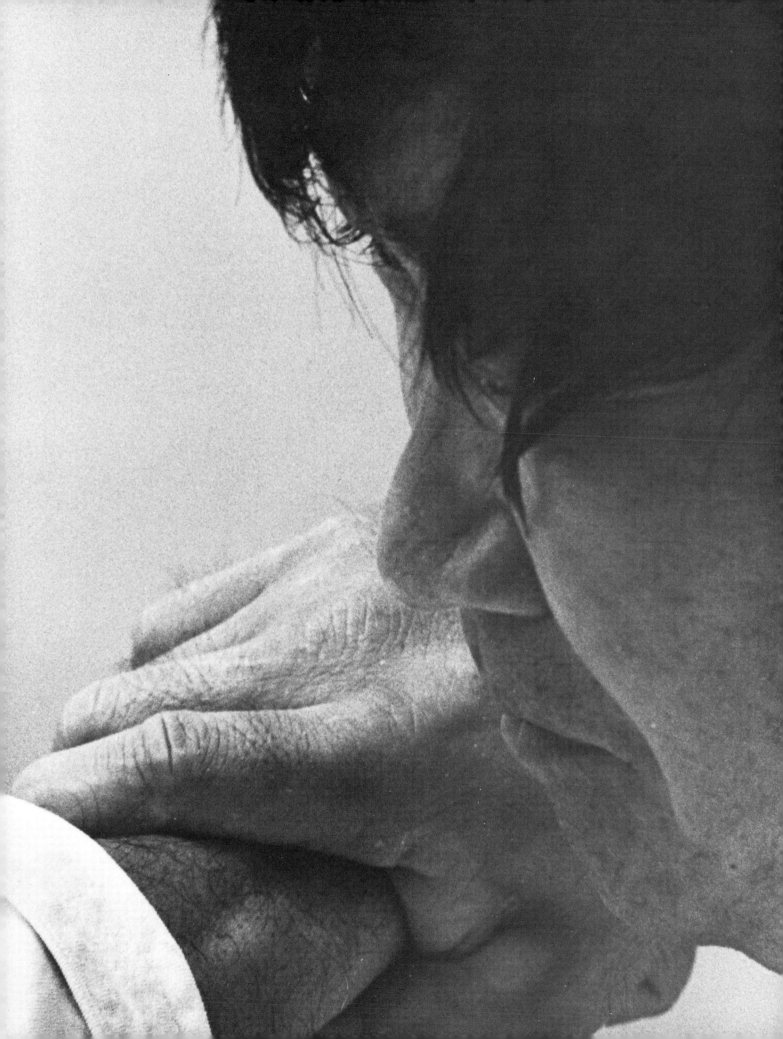

UKE NO KATA
Towards perfection of a defensive form

空の空道の型

海に空手道の四段の型

UMI TO KARATE-DO NO YODAN NO KATA
Movements of the kata should be as effortless as the tides

KARATE-DO UKE NO KATA
Defense form (outside blocking)

空手道学の型

MAEGERI UKE NO KATA
Blocking of front kick in kata form

KARATE GODAN NO KATA
A series of movements in the fifth kata (jumping over a weapon)

"The power of commitment is wondrous and can transcend
all other forces..."

横とび蹴

YOKO-TOBI KERI
Side thrust kick

澤道のとび上り練習

とぶ

TOBI AGARU
Jumping upward

二段後蹴

NIDAN ATO-GERI
Double jump kick

179

空手道と山の上

MAE GERI
Face kick

學道四～六段突

JYODAN TSUKI
Face punch

空手道の後屈立

KOKUTSU DACHI
The back stance – the weight is on the back leg, allowing
for added distance from the opponent

UKE
Double defense

空手の後屋立

KOKUTSU DACHI
Back stance

YO DAN NO UKE TO KAGE
Double open hand defense

四段の空手道の型

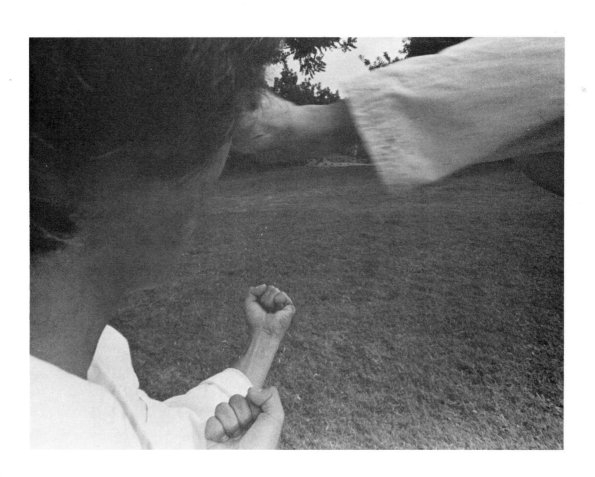

空手道中段突

CHUDAN TSUKI
Middle thrust punch (OIZUKE)

空手道史龍内受

CHUDAN UCHI-UKE
Outside defense

空道中段逆突

CHUDAN GYAKU-ZUKI
Reverse punch to the midsection

GODAN NO KATA
Jumping movement in the fifth form

UKE
Defense

空手道の礼

REI
Final bow

211

"The art of karate is a never ending quest for perfection...
of developing the spirit and the body to defeat your
opponent...one's self."

Appendix

Glossary

HAJIME—TO BEGIN

KARATE	Open hand
DOJO	School
SE IZA	Traditional sitting position for meditation
MOKUSO	Intensive meditation
SHO-MEN NI REI	A respectful bow to the dojo (school)
SHI-HAN NI REI	A respectful bow to the Master
O TA GAI NI REI	A respectful bow to another
SEM PAI NI REI	A respectful bow to your senior
KI-AI	A shout or yell "EI YA!", a manifestation of life forces in a burst of power
YA SU ME	The command for rest or at ease between exercises
SOJI	A mind discipline exercise involving the physical cleaning of something such as the dojo floor (This shows respect to the dojo)

TACHIKATA—STANDING FORMS & MOVEMENTS

ZEN-KU-TSU DACHI	Front stance
KO-KU-TSU DACHI	Back stance
HEI-SO-KU DACHI	Formal attention stance
MU-SU-BI DACHI	Informal attention stance
HEIKO-DACHI	Parallel stance
KI-BA DACHI	Riding horse stance
SHI-KO DACHI	Sumo stance (similar to KI-BA DACHI)
UCHI-MATA DACHI	Inverted foot stance
RE-DACHI	"L" stance
FU-DO DACHI	Rooted stance
SAN-CHIN DACHI	Inward tension stance
NEKO-ASHI	Cat foot stance
HAN-GETSU DACHI	Half moon stance

TSUKI—ATTACK FORMS

JYODAN TSUKI	Punch to upward area
CHUDAN TSUKI	Punch to middle area
GEDAN TSUKI	Punch to lower area
MAWASHI ZUKI	Round punch
OIZUKI	Stepping punch
NU KI TE	Finger thrust
SEI KEN	Fist thrust utilizing first two knuckles
TA TE ZU KI	Vertical fist punch
SHI YO TE UCHI	Striking with heel of hand
SHUTO UCHI	Knife hand strike
HAI TO UCHI	Striking with inside edge of hand
URA-KEN	Back fist
HIRA KEN	Forefinger knuckle
ITTPON ZUKI	One knuckle thrust
EM PI	Elbow
YOKO EMPI	Side elbow
TATE EMPI	Upward elbow
USHIRO EMPI	Back elbow
JYODAN EMPI	Elbow to upward area
GEDAN EMPI	Lower elbow attack
ZU ZU KI	Forehead attack
HIZA UCHI	Knee strike
ATAMA-YOKO UCHI	Side head strike
ATAMA-USHIRO UCHI	Backward head strike
MAKIWARA	Padded board used as a target for striking techniques

KERI—ATTACK KICKING FORMS

MAE GERI	Front kick

USHIRO GERI	Back kick	MOROTE UKE	Double hand block
MAWASHI GERI	Round kick	TSU-RU UKE	Crane block with top of wrist
YOKO GERI	Side kick		
MAE-KERI AGE	Front snapping kick	NI-JYU UKE	"X" block, cross of arms defense
YOKO-KERI AGE	Side snapping kick		
UCHI-MAWASHI GERI	Inside round kick	ASHI UKE	Shin block
SOTO-MAWASHI GERI	Outside round kick	TAI-SA-BAKI UKE	Evading block, defensive turn with no contact
MAE FUMIKOMI	Front stamping kick		
YOKO FUMIKOMI	Side stamping kick		
NANAME FUMIKOMI	45° stamping kick	ASHI-BARAI UKE	Foot sweep block
TO BI KERI	Jump kick	ASHI-NO-HIRA UKE	Bottom of foot block
YOKO TO BI KERI	Side jump kick	NA-GEN UKE	Throwing block (pick up opponent)
NI-DAN GERI	Double kick		
SAN-DAN GERI	Three direction kick	TO BI KERINO UKE	Jump kick block
SAN-KAKU TO BI KERI	Three-way jump kick	HIZA UKE	Knee block
TO BI-USHIRO GERI	Jumping back kick	U DE UKE	Forearm block

UKE—DEFENSIVE BLOCKING FORMS | SHIAI—TOURNAMENT CEREMONY

TA-O-RE GERI	Falling kick	TAIKAI	Championship
TSU-MASAKI GERI	Toe kick	SHO BU ARI	Winner
KA-GATO GERI	Heel kick	YAME	Command word meaning stop
SO-KUTO GERI	Side of foot kick		

UKE—DEFENSIVE BLOCKING FORMS____

JYODAN UKE	Upward block to protect neck with arm	SO RE MA DE	Finish
		REI	Bow
CHUDAN UKE	Middle block to protect midsection	O WARI	End of competition
		KUMITE	Sparring
GEDAN BARAI	Low block to protect groin area	ITTPON KUMITE	One-step movement
		NI-HON KUMITE	Two-step movement
CHUDAN-UCHI UKE	Middle inside block using wrist	SAN-BON KUMITE	Three-step movement
		ITTPON WAZA	One-step technique
CHUDAN-SOTO UKE	Middle outside block	WAZA	Technique
NAGASHI UKE	Sweeping block with legs		

[Publisher's Note: Shihan Tak Kubota knows over 2,000 wazas]

TO-ME UKE	Stopping block with forearms
HARAI UKE	Side-sweeping block
SHUTO UKE	Knife hand block
HAITO UKE	Inside ridge hand block

Advancement

The International Karate Association is a professional organization which instructs students of karate in over 100 dojos worldwide and sponsors teams in international competition. The I.K.A.'s criteria for recognizing student achievement is based on both spiritual and physical proficiency. A progression of "KYUs" or "grades" designating degrees of competence are used. These degrees are traditionally identified by color-coded ceremonial belts worn by each student.

After learning basic etiquette (see GLOSSARY under HAJIME), the student is assigned a "O" kyu and is allowed to wear a white belt. "6" kyu, the next grade, is a purple belt—"5" and "4" kyus, a green belt; "3", "2", and "1" kyus, a brown belt.

The student advances in designation according to his ability to perform the "KATAS", or "choreographed technique forms", to the Master's satisfaction. The kata is not merely a series of movements, but the challenge of combat without an opponent, thus producing a perfection in waiting—the grace, consciousness, coordination, and power of the physical self and spirit. The student becomes a "SHODAN", or "1st Degree" black belt, when he has successfully performed thirteen katas before the Master. The black belt designation progresses from a first to a fifth degree, at which point the student must be able to successfully perform twenty-one katas.

It is a common misconception that the black belt signifies the ultimate in karate expertise, perhaps because there have been few who have surpassed it. However, when a student reaches the level of a sixth degree black belt, he is allowed to wear a black belt with a red stripe. The ultimate designation of a person's ability is a red belt signifying an eighth to tenth degree proficiency level which is worn by perhaps three people in the world.

[Publisher's Note: Takiyuki Kubota is one of them.]

Acknowledgments

The author and publisher would like to thank the following individuals and organizations for their significant contributions to this effort...

For assistance to Shihan Kubota:
Vincent Matsudaira
Ben Otake
Gary Nakano
Dorsey Ito
Robert Shimokochi
Dennis Bedard
and the students and staff of the International Karate Association

For additional photography:
Steve Lesberg
Steven C. Sargeant

For photo laboratory services:
C.M. Photography
Santa Ana, California

Elaine Merrilees

For translation and editorial assistance:
Ann Miyake

For project design and coordination:
The Pacific Coast Creative Company
Corona del Mar, California

Alane Cochrane & Sharon Pittman – layout and production
Naomi Goldberg – administration and editorial
Steven C. Sargeant – design, layout, and coordination
Steve Lesberg – design, editorial, and coordination